Cycling
LOG BOOK

Belongs To

_____

_____

_____

Cycling LOG BOOK

Date _____

Start Time _____

End Time _____

Day Mon ○ Tue ○ Wed ○ Thu ○ Fri ○ Sat ○ Sun ○

Route

🚴 Total Distance	🕐 Total Time	🐢 Average Speed

Route Rating

Road Condition ☆ ☆ ☆ ☆ ☆

Difficulty ☆ ☆ ☆ ☆ ☆

Equipment Changes

Position Changes

Notes

Cycling LOG BOOK

Date _____

Start Time _____

End Time _____

Weather

🌡 ___

🎐 ___

☀ ⛅ ☁ 🌧 ❄

☐ ☐ ☐ ☐ ☐

Day Mon ○ Tue ○ Wed ○ Thu ○ Fri ○ Sat ○ Sun ○

Route

Total Distance	Total Time	Average Speed

Route Rating

Road Condition ☆ ☆ ☆ ☆ ☆

Difficulty ☆ ☆ ☆ ☆ ☆

Equipment Changes

Position Changes

Notes

Cycling LOG BOOK

Date _____

Start Time _____

End Time _____

Weather

Day Mon ○ Tue ○ Wed ○ Thu ○ Fri ○ Sat ○ Sun ○

Route

🚴 Total Distance	🕐 Total Time	☁ Average Speed

Route Rating

Road Condition ☆ ☆ ☆ ☆ ☆

Difficulty ☆ ☆ ☆ ☆ ☆

Equipment Changes

Position Changes

Notes

Cycling LOG BOOK

Date _____

Start Time _____

End Time _____

Weather

🌡 ___   ☀ ⛅ ☁ 🌧 ❄
🚩 ___   ☐ ☐ ☐ ☐ ☐

Day Mon○ Tue○ Wed○ Thu○ Fri○ Sat○ Sun○

Route

🐾 Total Distance	🕐 Total Time	☂ Average Speed

Route Rating

Road Condition ☆ ☆ ☆ ☆ ☆   Difficulty ☆ ☆ ☆ ☆ ☆

Equipment Changes

Position Changes

Notes

Cycling LOG BOOK

Date _____

Start Time _____

End Time _____

Day: Mon○   Tue○   Wed○   Thu○   Fri○   Sat○   Sun○

Route

🦶 Total Distance	🕐 Total Time	☁ Average Speed

Route Rating

Road Condition ☆ ☆ ☆ ☆ ☆   Difficulty ☆ ☆ ☆ ☆ ☆

Equipment Changes

Position Changes

Notes

Cycling LOG BOOK

Date _____

Start Time _____

End Time _____

Weather

🌡 —— ☀ ⛅ 🌧 ⛈ ❄

🚩 —— ☐ ☐ ☐ ☐ ☐

Day Mon ○ Tue ○ Wed ○ Thu ○ Fri ○ Sat ○ Sun ○

Route

🐾 Total Distance	🕐 Total Time	⛰ Average Speed

Route Rating

Road Condition ☆ ☆ ☆ ☆ ☆   Difficulty ☆ ☆ ☆ ☆ ☆

Equipment Changes

Position Changes

Notes

Cycling LOG BOOK

Date _____

Start Time _____

End Time _____

Day: Mon ○ Tue ○ Wed ○ Thu ○ Fri ○ Sat ○ Sun ○

Route

🦴 Total Distance	🕐 Total Time	△ Average Speed

Route Rating

Road Condition ☆ ☆ ☆ ☆ ☆   Difficulty ☆ ☆ ☆ ☆ ☆

Equipment Changes

Position Changes

Notes

Cycling LOG BOOK

Date _____

Weather

Start Time _____

End Time _____

Day Mon ○ Tue ○ Wed ○ Thu ○ Fri ○ Sat ○ Sun ○

Route

Total Distance	Total Time	Average Speed

Route Rating

Road Condition ☆ ☆ ☆ ☆ ☆

Difficulty ☆ ☆ ☆ ☆ ☆

Equipment Changes

Position Changes

Notes

Cycling LOG BOOK

Date _____

Start Time _____

End Time _____

Day Mon ○   Tue ○   Wed ○   Thu ○   Fri ○   Sat ○   Sun ○

Weather

Route

☙ Total Distance	◷ Total Time	☁ Average Speed

Route Rating

Road Condition ☆ ☆ ☆ ☆ ☆   Difficulty ☆ ☆ ☆ ☆ ☆

Equipment Changes

Position Changes

Notes

Cycling LOG BOOK

Date _____

Start Time _____

End Time _____

Weather

Day Mon ○ Tue ○ Wed ○ Thu ○ Fri ○ Sat ○ Sun ○

Route

🚲 Total Distance	🕐 Total Time	☁ Average Speed

Route Rating

Road Condition ☆ ☆ ☆ ☆ ☆   Difficulty ☆ ☆ ☆ ☆ ☆

Equipment Changes

Position Changes

Notes

Cycling LOG BOOK

Date _____

Start Time _____

End Time _____

Day Mon ○ Tue ○ Wed ○ Thu ○ Fri ○ Sat ○ Sun ○

Weather

🌡 ____   ☀ ⛅ ☁ 🌦 ❄
🚩 ____   ☐ ☐ ☐ ☐ ☐

Route

Total Distance	Total Time	Average Speed

Route Rating

Road Condition ☆ ☆ ☆ ☆ ☆   Difficulty ☆ ☆ ☆ ☆ ☆

Equipment Changes

Position Changes

Notes

Cycling LOG BOOK

Date _____

Weather

🌡 ___   ☀ ⛅ ☁ 🌧 ❄

🚩 ___   ☐ ☐ ☐ ☐ ☐

Start Time _____

End Time _____

Day Mon ○ Tue ○ Wed ○ Thu ○ Fri ○ Sat ○ Sun ○

Route

🐾 Total Distance	🕐 Total Time	🌂 Average Speed

Route Rating

Road Condition ☆ ☆ ☆ ☆ ☆

Difficulty ☆ ☆ ☆ ☆ ☆

Equipment Changes

Position Changes

Notes

Cycling LOG BOOK

Date _____

Start Time _____

End Time _____

Day Mon ○   Tue ○   Wed ○   Thu ○   Fri ○   Sat ○   Sun ○

Route

Total Distance

Total Time

Average Speed

Route Rating

Road Condition ☆ ☆ ☆ ☆ ☆

Difficulty ☆ ☆ ☆ ☆ ☆

Equipment Changes

Position Changes

Notes

Cycling LOG BOOK

Date _____

Start Time _____

End Time _____

Day: Mon ○ Tue ○ Wed ○ Thu ○ Fri ○ Sat ○ Sun ○

Weather

🌡 _____   ☀ ⛅ 🌧 ⛈ ❄

🎏 _____   ☐ ☐ ☐ ☐ ☐

Route

Total Distance	Total Time	Average Speed

Route Rating

Road Condition ☆ ☆ ☆ ☆ ☆   Difficulty ☆ ☆ ☆ ☆ ☆

Equipment Changes

Position Changes

Notes

Cycling LOG BOOK

Date _____

Weather

Start Time _____

End Time _____

Day Mon ○ Tue ○ Wed ○ Thu ○ Fri ○ Sat ○ Sun ○

Route

🐾 Total Distance	🕐 Total Time	◠ Average Speed

Route Rating

Road Condition ☆ ☆ ☆ ☆ ☆

Difficulty ☆ ☆ ☆ ☆ ☆

Equipment Changes

Position Changes

Notes

Cycling LOG BOOK

Date _____

Weather

Start Time _____

End Time _____

Day Mon ○   Tue ○   Wed ○   Thu ○   Fri ○   Sat ○   Sun ○

Route

🐾 Total Distance	🕐 Total Time	☁ Average Speed

Route Rating

Road Condition ☆ ☆ ☆ ☆ ☆   Difficulty ☆ ☆ ☆ ☆ ☆

Equipment Changes

Position Changes

Notes

Cycling LOG BOOK

Date _____

Start Time _____

End Time _____

Weather

🌡 —   ☀ ⛅ ☁ 🌧 ❄

🚩 —   ☐ ☐ ☐ ☐ ☐

Day: Mon○ Tue○ Wed○ Thu○ Fri○ Sat○ Sun○

Route

🐾 Total Distance	🕐 Total Time	☁ Average Speed

Route Rating

Road Condition ☆☆☆☆☆   Difficulty ☆☆☆☆☆

Equipment Changes

Position Changes

Notes

Cycling LOG BOOK

Date _____

Weather

🌡 ___ ☀ ⛅ ☁ 🌧 ❄

🏳 ___ ☐ ☐ ☐ ☐ ☐

Start Time _____

End Time _____

Day Mon○ Tue○ Wed○ Thu○ Fri○ Sat○ Sun○

Route

🚲 Total Distance	🕐 Total Time	🌡 Average Speed

Route Rating

Road Condition ☆ ☆ ☆ ☆ ☆   Difficulty ☆ ☆ ☆ ☆ ☆

Equipment Changes

Position Changes

Notes

Cycling LOG BOOK

Date _____

Start Time _____

End Time _____

Day Mon◯ Tue◯ Wed◯ Thu◯ Fri◯ Sat◯ Sun◯

Route

⛓Total Distance	🕐 Total Time	☁ Average Speed

Route Rating

Road Condition ☆ ☆ ☆ ☆ ☆   Difficulty ☆ ☆ ☆ ☆ ☆

Equipment Changes

Position Changes

Notes

Cycling LOG BOOK

Date _____

Weather

Start Time _____

End Time _____

Day Mon ○ Tue ○ Wed ○ Thu ○ Fri ○ Sat ○ Sun ○

Route

Total Distance	Total Time	Average Speed

Route Rating

Road Condition ☆ ☆ ☆ ☆ ☆   Difficulty ☆ ☆ ☆ ☆ ☆

Equipment Changes

Position Changes

Notes

Cycling LOG BOOK

Date _____

Start Time _____

End Time _____

Weather

🌡 ____   ☀ ⛅ ☁ ⛈ ❄

🚩 ____   ☐ ☐ ☐ ☐ ☐

Day Mon ○ Tue ○ Wed ○ Thu ○ Fri ○ Sat ○ Sun ○

Route

🚲 Total Distance

🕐 Total Time

🌡 Average Speed

Route Rating

Road Condition ☆ ☆ ☆ ☆ ☆   Difficulty ☆ ☆ ☆ ☆ ☆

Equipment Changes

Position Changes

Notes

Cycling LOG BOOK

Date _____

Start Time _____

End Time _____

Day Mon ○   Tue ○   Wed ○   Thu ○   Fri ○   Sat ○   Sun ○

Route

Total Distance	Total Time	Average Speed

Route Rating

Road Condition ☆ ☆ ☆ ☆ ☆   Difficulty ☆ ☆ ☆ ☆ ☆

Equipment Changes

Position Changes

Notes

Cycling LOG BOOK

Date _____

Start Time _____

End Time _____

Weather

Day Mon ○   Tue ○   Wed ○   Thu ○   Fri ○   Sat ○   Sun ○

Route

☙ Total Distance	🕐 Total Time	☁ Average Speed

Route Rating

Road Condition ☆ ☆ ☆ ☆ ☆

Difficulty ☆ ☆ ☆ ☆ ☆

Equipment Changes

Position Changes

Notes

Cycling LOG BOOK

Date _____

Start Time _____

End Time _____

Weather

Day Mon◯ Tue◯ Wed◯ Thu◯ Fri◯ Sat◯ Sun◯

Route

🦶 Total Distance	🕐 Total Time	☁ Average Speed

Route Rating

Road Condition ☆ ☆ ☆ ☆ ☆   Difficulty ☆ ☆ ☆ ☆ ☆

Equipment Changes

Position Changes

Notes

Cycling LOG BOOK

Date _____

Start Time _____

End Time _____

Day: Mon ○ Tue ○ Wed ○ Thu ○ Fri ○ Sat ○ Sun ○

Weather

🌡 ____ ☀ 🌤 🌧 ⛈ ❄

🚩 ____ ☐ ☐ ☐ ☐ ☐

Route

🚴 Total Distance	🕐 Total Time	△ Average Speed

Route Rating

Road Condition ☆ ☆ ☆ ☆ ☆   Difficulty ☆ ☆ ☆ ☆ ☆

Equipment Changes

Position Changes

Notes

Cycling LOG BOOK

Date _____

Weather

Start Time _____

End Time _____

Day Mon ○   Tue ○   Wed ○   Thu ○   Fri ○   Sat ○   Sun ○

Route

🌀 Total Distance	🕐 Total Time	☁ Average Speed

Route Rating

Road Condition ☆ ☆ ☆ ☆ ☆   Difficulty ☆ ☆ ☆ ☆ ☆

Equipment Changes

Position Changes

Notes

Cycling LOG BOOK

Date _____

Start Time _____

End Time _____

Weather

Day Mon ○ Tue ○ Wed ○ Thu ○ Fri ○ Sat ○ Sun ○

Route

Total Distance	Total Time	Average Speed

Route Rating

Road Condition ☆ ☆ ☆ ☆ ☆   Difficulty ☆ ☆ ☆ ☆ ☆

Equipment Changes

Position Changes

Notes

Cycling LOG BOOK

Date _____

Start Time _____

End Time _____

Weather

Day Mon ○   Tue ○   Wed ○   Thu ○   Fri ○   Sat ○   Sun ○

Route

Total Distance	Total Time	Average Speed

Route Rating

Road Condition ☆ ☆ ☆ ☆ ☆   Difficulty ☆ ☆ ☆ ☆ ☆

Equipment Changes

Position Changes

Notes

Cycling LOG BOOK

Date _____

Start Time _____

End Time _____

Weather

🌡 ____ ☀ ⛅ ☁ 🌦 ❄

🚩 ____ ☐ ☐ ☐ ☐ ☐

Day Mon ○ Tue ○ Wed ○ Thu ○ Fri ○ Sat ○ Sun ○

Route

🐾 Total Distance	🕐 Total Time	☁ Average Speed

Route Rating

Road Condition ☆ ☆ ☆ ☆ ☆   Difficulty ☆ ☆ ☆ ☆ ☆

Equipment Changes

Position Changes

Notes

Cycling LOG BOOK

Date _____

Start Time _____

End Time _____

Weather

Day Mon ○ Tue ○ Wed ○ Thu ○ Fri ○ Sat ○ Sun ○

Route

🦶 Total Distance	🕐 Total Time	🌡 Average Speed

Route Rating

Road Condition ☆ ☆ ☆ ☆ ☆   Difficulty ☆ ☆ ☆ ☆ ☆

Equipment Changes

Position Changes

Notes

Cycling LOG BOOK

Date _____

Start Time _____

End Time _____

Day Mon ○   Tue ○   Wed ○   Thu ○   Fri ○   Sat ○   Sun ○

Weather

Route

🐾 Total Distance	🕐 Total Time	🌡 Average Speed

Route Rating

Road Condition ☆ ☆ ☆ ☆ ☆

Difficulty ☆ ☆ ☆ ☆ ☆

Equipment Changes

Position Changes

Notes

Cycling LOG BOOK

Date _____

Start Time _____

End Time _____

Weather

Day Mon○ Tue○ Wed○ Thu○ Fri○ Sat○ Sun○

Route

🦶Total Distance	🕐 Total Time	🌡 Average Speed

Route Rating

Road Condition ☆ ☆ ☆ ☆ ☆

Difficulty ☆ ☆ ☆ ☆ ☆

Equipment Changes

Position Changes

Notes

Cycling LOG BOOK

Date _____

Start Time _____

End Time _____

Weather

Day Mon ○ Tue ○ Wed ○ Thu ○ Fri ○ Sat ○ Sun ○

Route

✤ Total Distance	🕐 Total Time	☁ Average Speed

Route Rating

Road Condition ☆ ☆ ☆ ☆ ☆

Difficulty ☆ ☆ ☆ ☆ ☆

Equipment Changes

Position Changes

Notes

Cycling LOG BOOK

Date _____

Start Time _____

End Time _____

Day: Mon ○ Tue ○ Wed ○ Thu ○ Fri ○ Sat ○ Sun ○

Weather

🌡 ___   ☀ ⛅ 🌧 ⛈ ❄

🏳 ___   ☐ ☐ ☐ ☐ ☐

Route

🚴 Total Distance

⏱ Total Time

🔺 Average Speed

Route Rating

Road Condition ☆ ☆ ☆ ☆ ☆

Difficulty ☆ ☆ ☆ ☆ ☆

Equipment Changes

Position Changes

Notes

Cycling LOG BOOK

Date _____

Weather

Start Time _____

End Time _____

Day: Mon ○ Tue ○ Wed ○ Thu ○ Fri ○ Sat ○ Sun ○

Route

Total Distance	Total Time	Average Speed

Route Rating

Road Condition ☆ ☆ ☆ ☆ ☆

Difficulty ☆ ☆ ☆ ☆ ☆

Equipment Changes

Position Changes

Notes

Cycling LOG BOOK

Date _____

Start Time _____

End Time _____

Weather

🌡 ____ ☀ ⛅ ☁ 🌧 ❄

🎐 ____ ☐ ☐ ☐ ☐ ☐

Day Mon ○ Tue ○ Wed ○ Thu ○ Fri ○ Sat ○ Sun ○

Route

🚲 Total Distance	🕐 Total Time	⏱ Average Speed

Route Rating

Road Condition ☆ ☆ ☆ ☆ ☆   Difficulty ☆ ☆ ☆ ☆ ☆

Equipment Changes

Position Changes

Notes

Cycling LOG BOOK

Date _____

Start Time _____

End Time _____

Weather

Day: Mon ○ Tue ○ Wed ○ Thu ○ Fri ○ Sat ○ Sun ○

Route

Total Distance	Total Time	Average Speed

Route Rating

Road Condition ☆ ☆ ☆ ☆ ☆

Difficulty ☆ ☆ ☆ ☆ ☆

Equipment Changes

Position Changes

Notes

Cycling LOG BOOK

Date _____

Weather

Start Time _____

End Time _____

Day Mon○ Tue○ Wed○ Thu○ Fri○ Sat○ Sun○

Route

🔄 Total Distance	🕐 Total Time	⌂ Average Speed

Route Rating

Road Condition ☆☆☆☆☆   Difficulty ☆☆☆☆☆

Equipment Changes

Position Changes

Notes

Cycling LOG BOOK

Date _____

Weather

🌡 ___ ☀ ⛅ ☁ 🌧 ❄

🚩 ___ ☐ ☐ ☐ ☐ ☐

Start Time _____

End Time _____

Day Mon ○ Tue ○ Wed ○ Thu ○ Fri ○ Sat ○ Sun ○

Route

🔗 Total Distance	🕐 Total Time	🌂 Average Speed

Route Rating

Road Condition ☆ ☆ ☆ ☆ ☆

Difficulty ☆ ☆ ☆ ☆ ☆

Equipment Changes

Position Changes

Notes

Cycling LOG BOOK

Date _____

Weather

Start Time _____

End Time _____

Day Mon ○ Tue ○ Wed ○ Thu ○ Fri ○ Sat ○ Sun ○

Route

🚲 Total Distance	🕐 Total Time	☁ Average Speed

Route Rating

Road Condition ☆ ☆ ☆ ☆ ☆   Difficulty ☆ ☆ ☆ ☆ ☆

Equipment Changes

Position Changes

Notes

Cycling LOG BOOK

Date _____

Start Time _____

End Time _____

Weather

🌡 —   ☀ ⛅ ☁ 🌧 ❄
🚩 —   ☐ ☐ ☐ ☐ ☐

Day Mon ○   Tue ○   Wed ○   Thu ○   Fri ○   Sat ○   Sun ○

Route

🚴 Total Distance	🕐 Total Time	🌥 Average Speed

Route Rating

Road Condition ☆ ☆ ☆ ☆ ☆   Difficulty ☆ ☆ ☆ ☆ ☆

Equipment Changes

Position Changes

Notes

Cycling LOG BOOK

Date _____

Start Time _____

End Time _____

Day Mon ○ Tue ○ Wed ○ Thu ○ Fri ○ Sat ○ Sun ○

Weather

Route

🐾 Total Distance	🕐 Total Time	☁ Average Speed

Route Rating

Road Condition ☆ ☆ ☆ ☆ ☆   Difficulty ☆ ☆ ☆ ☆ ☆

Equipment Changes

Position Changes

Notes

Cycling LOG BOOK

Date _____

Start Time _____

End Time _____

Weather

Day: Mon ○ Tue ○ Wed ○ Thu ○ Fri ○ Sat ○ Sun ○

Route

🚲 Total Distance	🕐 Total Time	🕵 Average Speed

Route Rating

Road Condition ☆ ☆ ☆ ☆ ☆

Difficulty ☆ ☆ ☆ ☆ ☆

Equipment Changes

Position Changes

Notes

Cycling LOG BOOK

Date _____

Start Time _____

End Time _____

Day: Mon ○ Tue ○ Wed ○ Thu ○ Fri ○ Sat ○ Sun ○

Weather

Route

🔾 Total Distance	🕐 Total Time	⌂ Average Speed

Route Rating

Road Condition ☆ ☆ ☆ ☆ ☆   Difficulty ☆ ☆ ☆ ☆ ☆

Equipment Changes

Position Changes

Notes

Cycling LOG BOOK

Date _____

Weather

Start Time _____

End Time _____

Day Mon ○ Tue ○ Wed ○ Thu ○ Fri ○ Sat ○ Sun ○

Route

Total Distance

Total Time

Average Speed

Route Rating

Road Condition ☆ ☆ ☆ ☆ ☆

Difficulty ☆ ☆ ☆ ☆ ☆

Equipment Changes

Position Changes

Notes

Cycling LOG BOOK

Date _____

Start Time _____

End Time _____

Weather

Day Mon ○   Tue ○   Wed ○   Thu ○   Fri ○   Sat ○   Sun ○

Route

🚲 Total Distance	🕐 Total Time	🗻 Average Speed

Route Rating

Road Condition ☆ ☆ ☆ ☆ ☆   Difficulty ☆ ☆ ☆ ☆ ☆

Equipment Changes

Position Changes

Notes

Cycling LOG BOOK

Date _____

Start Time _____

End Time _____

Weather

Day   Mon ○   Tue ○   Wed ○   Thu ○   Fri ○   Sat ○   Sun ○

Route

Total Distance	Total Time	Average Speed

Route Rating

Road Condition ☆ ☆ ☆ ☆ ☆

Difficulty ☆ ☆ ☆ ☆ ☆

Equipment Changes

Position Changes

Notes

Cycling LOG BOOK

Date _____

Start Time _____

End Time _____

Weather

🌡 ———   ☀ ⛅ ☁ 🌧 ❄

🎐 ———   ☐ ☐ ☐ ☐ ☐

Day Mon ○   Tue ○   Wed ○   Thu ○   Fri ○   Sat ○   Sun ○

Route

🐾 Total Distance

⏲ Total Time

☁ Average Speed

Route Rating

Road Condition ☆ ☆ ☆ ☆ ☆

Difficulty ☆ ☆ ☆ ☆ ☆

Equipment Changes

Position Changes

Notes

Cycling LOG BOOK

Date _____

Weather

🌡 ___ ☀ ⛅ 🌧 ⛆ ❄

🚩 ___ ☐ ☐ ☐ ☐ ☐

Start Time _____

End Time _____

Day Mon ○ Tue ○ Wed ○ Thu ○ Fri ○ Sat ○ Sun ○

Route

🚴 Total Distance	⏱ Total Time	🌡 Average Speed

Route Rating

Road Condition ☆ ☆ ☆ ☆ ☆   Difficulty ☆ ☆ ☆ ☆ ☆

Equipment Changes

Position Changes

Notes

Cycling LOG BOOK

Date _____

Start Time _____

End Time _____

Weather

Day Mon ○   Tue ○   Wed ○   Thu ○   Fri ○   Sat ○   Sun ○

Route

🐾 Total Distance	🕐 Total Time	☁ Average Speed

Route Rating

Road Condition ☆ ☆ ☆ ☆ ☆   Difficulty ☆ ☆ ☆ ☆ ☆

Equipment Changes

Position Changes

Notes

Cycling LOG BOOK

Date _____

Weather

Start Time _____

End Time _____

Day Mon ○ Tue ○ Wed ○ Thu ○ Fri ○ Sat ○ Sun ○

Route

🐾 Total Distance	🕐 Total Time	☂ Average Speed

Route Rating

Road Condition ☆ ☆ ☆ ☆ ☆   Difficulty ☆ ☆ ☆ ☆ ☆

Equipment Changes

Position Changes

Notes

Cycling LOG BOOK

Date _____

Start Time _____

End Time _____

Weather

Day Mon○ Tue○ Wed○ Thu○ Fri○ Sat○ Sun○

Route

🚲 Total Distance	🕐 Total Time	☁ Average Speed

Route Rating

Road Condition ☆ ☆ ☆ ☆ ☆

Difficulty ☆ ☆ ☆ ☆ ☆

Equipment Changes

Position Changes

Notes

Cycling LOG BOOK

Date _____

Start Time _____

End Time _____

Day Mon ○ Tue ○ Wed ○ Thu ○ Fri ○ Sat ○ Sun ○

Route

Total Distance	Total Time	Average Speed

Route Rating

Road Condition ☆ ☆ ☆ ☆ ☆   Difficulty ☆ ☆ ☆ ☆ ☆

Equipment Changes

Position Changes

Notes

Cycling LOG BOOK

Date _____

Start Time _____

End Time _____

Weather

Day: Mon ○ Tue ○ Wed ○ Thu ○ Fri ○ Sat ○ Sun ○

Route

🚲 Total Distance	🕐 Total Time	⛰ Average Speed

Route Rating

Road Condition ☆ ☆ ☆ ☆ ☆   Difficulty ☆ ☆ ☆ ☆ ☆

Equipment Changes

Position Changes

Notes

Cycling LOG BOOK

Date _____

Weather

Start Time _____

End Time _____

Day Mon ○ Tue ○ Wed ○ Thu ○ Fri ○ Sat ○ Sun ○

Route

⛄ Total Distance	🕐 Total Time	🌂 Average Speed

Route Rating

Road Condition ☆ ☆ ☆ ☆ ☆

Difficulty ☆ ☆ ☆ ☆ ☆

Equipment Changes

Position Changes

Notes

Cycling LOG BOOK

Date _____

Start Time _____

End Time _____

Weather

Day Mon ○ Tue ○ Wed ○ Thu ○ Fri ○ Sat ○ Sun ○

Route

Total Distance	Total Time	Average Speed

Route Rating

Road Condition ☆ ☆ ☆ ☆ ☆   Difficulty ☆ ☆ ☆ ☆ ☆

Equipment Changes

Position Changes

Notes

Cycling LOG BOOK

Date _____

Start Time _____

End Time _____

Weather

🌡 — ☀ ⛅ 🌧 ⛈ ❄

🚩 — ☐ ☐ ☐ ☐ ☐

Day Mon ○ Tue ○ Wed ○ Thu ○ Fri ○ Sat ○ Sun ○

Route

Total Distance

Total Time

Average Speed

Route Rating

Road Condition ☆ ☆ ☆ ☆ ☆

Difficulty ☆ ☆ ☆ ☆ ☆

Equipment Changes

Position Changes

Notes

Cycling LOG BOOK

Date _____

Weather

Start Time _____

End Time _____

Day Mon ○ Tue ○ Wed ○ Thu ○ Fri ○ Sat ○ Sun ○

Route

🚲 Total Distance	🕐 Total Time	⌓ Average Speed

Route Rating

Road Condition ☆ ☆ ☆ ☆ ☆

Difficulty ☆ ☆ ☆ ☆ ☆

Equipment Changes

Position Changes

Notes

Cycling LOG BOOK

Date _____

Start Time _____

End Time _____

Day: Mon ○ Tue ○ Wed ○ Thu ○ Fri ○ Sat ○ Sun ○

Weather

🌡 ___ ☀ ⛅ 🌧 ⛈ ❄

🚩 ___ ☐ ☐ ☐ ☐ ☐

Route

🚲 Total Distance	🕐 Total Time	☁ Average Speed

Route Rating

Road Condition ☆ ☆ ☆ ☆ ☆

Difficulty ☆ ☆ ☆ ☆ ☆

Equipment Changes

Position Changes

Notes

Cycling LOG BOOK

Date _____

Start Time _____

End Time _____

🌡 ___   ☀ ⛅ 🌧 ⛈ ❄

🏳 ___   ☐ ☐ ☐ ☐ ☐

Day Mon ○   Tue ○   Wed ○   Thu ○   Fri ○   Sat ○   Sun ○

Route

🚴 Total Distance	⏱ Total Time	🌡 Average Speed

Route Rating

Road Condition ☆ ☆ ☆ ☆ ☆   Difficulty ☆ ☆ ☆ ☆ ☆

Equipment Changes

Position Changes

Notes

Cycling LOG BOOK

Date _____

Start Time _____

End Time _____

Day Mon ○   Tue ○   Wed ○   Thu ○   Fri ○   Sat ○   Sun ○

Weather

🌡 ___   ☀   ⛅   🌧   ⛈   ❄
🚩 ___   ☐   ☐   ☐   ☐   ☐

Route

🚴 Total Distance	🕐 Total Time	🕣 Average Speed

Route Rating

Road Condition ☆ ☆ ☆ ☆ ☆   Difficulty ☆ ☆ ☆ ☆ ☆

Equipment Changes

Position Changes

Notes

Cycling LOG BOOK

Date _____

Start Time _____

End Time _____

Weather

Day: Mon ○ Tue ○ Wed ○ Thu ○ Fri ○ Sat ○ Sun ○

Route

🐾 Total Distance	🕐 Total Time	🛆 Average Speed

Route Rating

Road Condition ☆ ☆ ☆ ☆ ☆   Difficulty ☆ ☆ ☆ ☆ ☆

Equipment Changes

Position Changes

Notes

Cycling LOG BOOK

Date _____

Start Time _____

End Time _____

Weather

Day Mon○ Tue○ Wed○ Thu○ Fri○ Sat○ Sun○

Route

🚲 Total Distance	🕐 Total Time	⌓ Average Speed

Route Rating

Road Condition ☆ ☆ ☆ ☆ ☆

Difficulty ☆ ☆ ☆ ☆ ☆

Equipment Changes

Position Changes

Notes

Cycling LOG BOOK

Date _____

Start Time _____

End Time _____

Weather

Day Mon○ Tue○ Wed○ Thu○ Fri○ Sat○ Sun○

Route

🚴 Total Distance	🕐 Total Time	⌂ Average Speed

Route Rating

Road Condition ☆ ☆ ☆ ☆ ☆   Difficulty ☆ ☆ ☆ ☆ ☆

Equipment Changes

Position Changes

Notes

Cycling LOG BOOK

Date _____

Start Time _____

End Time _____

Weather

Day: Mon ○ Tue ○ Wed ○ Thu ○ Fri ○ Sat ○ Sun ○

Route

🐾 Total Distance	🕐 Total Time	⛑ Average Speed

Route Rating

Road Condition ☆ ☆ ☆ ☆ ☆   Difficulty ☆ ☆ ☆ ☆ ☆

Equipment Changes

Position Changes

Notes

Cycling LOG BOOK

Date _____

Weather

Start Time _____

End Time _____

Day Mon ○   Tue ○   Wed ○   Thu ○   Fri ○   Sat ○   Sun ○

Route

Total Distance	Total Time	Average Speed

Route Rating

Road Condition ☆ ☆ ☆ ☆ ☆

Difficulty ☆ ☆ ☆ ☆ ☆

Equipment Changes

Position Changes

Notes

Cycling LOG BOOK

Date _____

Start Time _____

End Time _____

Weather

🌡 ——— ☀ ⛅ 🌧 ⛈ ❄

🚩 ——— ☐ ☐ ☐ ☐ ☐

Day Mon ○ Tue ○ Wed ○ Thu ○ Fri ○ Sat ○ Sun ○

Route

🚲 Total Distance	🕐 Total Time	⏱ Average Speed

Route Rating

Road Condition ☆ ☆ ☆ ☆ ☆   Difficulty ☆ ☆ ☆ ☆ ☆

Equipment Changes

Position Changes

Notes

$\mathcal{C}ycling$ LOG BOOK

Date _____

Weather

Start Time _____

End Time _____

Day Mon ○ Tue ○ Wed ○ Thu ○ Fri ○ Sat ○ Sun ○

Route

Total Distance	Total Time	Average Speed

Route Rating

Road Condition ☆ ☆ ☆ ☆ ☆   Difficulty ☆ ☆ ☆ ☆ ☆

Equipment Changes

Position Changes

Notes

Cycling LOG BOOK

Date _____

Start Time _____

End Time _____

Weather

🌡 —— ☀ ⛅ ☁ 🌧 ❄

🚩 —— ☐ ☐ ☐ ☐ ☐

Day Mon◯ Tue◯ Wed◯ Thu◯ Fri◯ Sat◯ Sun◯

Route

🐾 Total Distance	🕐 Total Time	🛡 Average Speed

Route Rating

Road Condition ☆ ☆ ☆ ☆ ☆   Difficulty ☆ ☆ ☆ ☆ ☆

Equipment Changes

Position Changes

Notes

Cycling LOG BOOK

Date _____

Start Time _____

End Time _____

Weather

Day Mon ○ Tue ○ Wed ○ Thu ○ Fri ○ Sat ○ Sun ○

Route

🚲 Total Distance	🕐 Total Time	⌂ Average Speed

Route Rating

Road Condition ☆ ☆ ☆ ☆ ☆   Difficulty ☆ ☆ ☆ ☆ ☆

Equipment Changes

Position Changes

Notes

Cycling LOG BOOK

Date _____

Start Time _____

End Time _____

Day Mon ○ Tue ○ Wed ○ Thu ○ Fri ○ Sat ○ Sun ○

Route

🚴 Total Distance	🕐 Total Time	🌡 Average Speed

Route Rating

Road Condition ☆ ☆ ☆ ☆ ☆   Difficulty ☆ ☆ ☆ ☆ ☆

Equipment Changes

Position Changes

Notes

Cycling LOG BOOK

Date _____

Weather

Start Time _____

End Time _____

Day Mon○ Tue○ Wed○ Thu○ Fri○ Sat○ Sun○

Route

🦶 Total Distance	🕐 Total Time	⌂ Average Speed

Route Rating

Road Condition ☆ ☆ ☆ ☆ ☆

Difficulty ☆ ☆ ☆ ☆ ☆

Equipment Changes

Position Changes

Notes

Cycling LOG BOOK

Date _____

Weather

Start Time _____

End Time _____

Day Mon ○ Tue ○ Wed ○ Thu ○ Fri ○ Sat ○ Sun ○

Route

☘ Total Distance	⏲ Total Time	⌓ Average Speed

Route Rating

Road Condition ☆ ☆ ☆ ☆ ☆   Difficulty ☆ ☆ ☆ ☆ ☆

Equipment Changes

Position Changes

Notes

Cycling LOG BOOK

Date _____

Start Time _____

End Time _____

Day Mon ○ Tue ○ Wed ○ Thu ○ Fri ○ Sat ○ Sun ○

Weather

| 🌡 | — | ☀ | ⛅ | 🌧 | ⛈ | ❄ |
| 🚩 | — | ☐ | ☐ | ☐ | ☐ | ☐ |

Route

🚴 Total Distance	🕐 Total Time	☁ Average Speed

Route Rating

Road Condition ☆ ☆ ☆ ☆ ☆   Difficulty ☆ ☆ ☆ ☆ ☆

Equipment Changes

Position Changes

Notes

Cycling LOG BOOK

Date _____

Start Time _____

End Time _____

Weather

Day Mon ○ Tue ○ Wed ○ Thu ○ Fri ○ Sat ○ Sun ○

Route

Total Distance	Total Time	Average Speed

Route Rating

Road Condition ☆ ☆ ☆ ☆ ☆   Difficulty ☆ ☆ ☆ ☆ ☆

Equipment Changes

Position Changes

Notes

Cycling LOG BOOK

Date _____

Start Time _____

End Time _____

Weather

Day Mon ○ Tue ○ Wed ○ Thu ○ Fri ○ Sat ○ Sun ○

Route

Total Distance	Total Time	Average Speed

Route Rating

Road Condition ☆ ☆ ☆ ☆ ☆   Difficulty ☆ ☆ ☆ ☆ ☆

Equipment Changes

Position Changes

Notes

Cycling LOG BOOK

Date _____

Start Time _____

End Time _____

Weather

Day: Mon ○ Tue ○ Wed ○ Thu ○ Fri ○ Sat ○ Sun ○

Route

🐾 Total Distance	🕐 Total Time	🌡 Average Speed

Route Rating

Road Condition ☆ ☆ ☆ ☆ ☆

Difficulty ☆ ☆ ☆ ☆ ☆

Equipment Changes

Position Changes

Notes

Cycling LOG BOOK

Date _____

Start Time _____

End Time _____

Day Mon ○ Tue ○ Wed ○ Thu ○ Fri ○ Sat ○ Sun ○

Route

🦶 Total Distance	🕐 Total Time	⏱ Average Speed

Route Rating

Road Condition ☆ ☆ ☆ ☆ ☆   Difficulty ☆ ☆ ☆ ☆ ☆

Equipment Changes

Position Changes

Notes

Cycling LOG BOOK

Date _____

Start Time _____

End Time _____

Day: Mon ○ Tue ○ Wed ○ Thu ○ Fri ○ Sat ○ Sun ○

Weather

Route

⚙ Total Distance	⏱ Total Time	⌂ Average Speed

Route Rating

Road Condition ☆ ☆ ☆ ☆ ☆   Difficulty ☆ ☆ ☆ ☆ ☆

Equipment Changes

Position Changes

Notes

Cycling LOG BOOK

Date _____

Start Time _____

End Time _____

Weather

Day Mon ○　Tue ○　Wed ○　Thu ○　Fri ○　Sat ○　Sun ○

Route

Total Distance	Total Time	Average Speed

Route Rating

Road Condition ☆ ☆ ☆ ☆ ☆　　　　Difficulty ☆ ☆ ☆ ☆ ☆

Equipment Changes

Position Changes

Notes

Cycling LOG BOOK

Date _____

Start Time _____

End Time _____

Weather

🌡 — ☀ ⛅ ☁ 🌧 ❄

🚩 — ☐ ☐ ☐ ☐ ☐

Day Mon○ Tue○ Wed○ Thu○ Fri○ Sat○ Sun○

Route

🐾 Total Distance	🕐 Total Time	🌡 Average Speed

Route Rating

Road Condition ☆ ☆ ☆ ☆ ☆   Difficulty ☆ ☆ ☆ ☆ ☆

Equipment Changes

Position Changes

Notes

Cycling LOG BOOK

Date _____

Start Time _____

End Time _____

Day Mon ○ Tue ○ Wed ○ Thu ○ Fri ○ Sat ○ Sun ○

Weather

Route

🚴 Total Distance	🕐 Total Time	☁ Average Speed

Route Rating

Road Condition ☆ ☆ ☆ ☆ ☆   Difficulty ☆ ☆ ☆ ☆ ☆

Equipment Changes

Position Changes

Notes

Cycling LOG BOOK

Date _____

Start Time _____

End Time _____

Weather

🌡 ____   ☀ ⛅ 🌧 ⛈ ❄
🚩 ____   ☐ ☐ ☐ ☐ ☐

Day: Mon ○ Tue ○ Wed ○ Thu ○ Fri ○ Sat ○ Sun ○

Route

Total Distance	Total Time	Average Speed

Route Rating

Road Condition ☆ ☆ ☆ ☆ ☆   Difficulty ☆ ☆ ☆ ☆ ☆

Equipment Changes

Position Changes

Notes

Cycling LOG BOOK

Date _____

Weather

Start Time _____

End Time _____

Day Mon ○ Tue ○ Wed ○ Thu ○ Fri ○ Sat ○ Sun ○

Route

🦶 Total Distance	🕐 Total Time	⛰ Average Speed

Route Rating

Road Condition ☆ ☆ ☆ ☆ ☆   Difficulty ☆ ☆ ☆ ☆ ☆

Equipment Changes

Position Changes

Notes

Cycling LOG BOOK

Date _____

Start Time _____

End Time _____

Day Mon○ Tue○ Wed○ Thu○ Fri○ Sat○ Sun○

Route

🦶 Total Distance	🕐 Total Time	🦫 Average Speed

Route Rating

Road Condition ☆ ☆ ☆ ☆ ☆   Difficulty ☆ ☆ ☆ ☆ ☆

Equipment Changes

Position Changes

Notes

Cycling LOG BOOK

Date _____

Start Time _____

End Time _____

Weather

Day Mon ○ Tue ○ Wed ○ Thu ○ Fri ○ Sat ○ Sun ○

Route

⚲ Total Distance	🕐 Total Time	☁ Average Speed

Route Rating

Road Condition ☆ ☆ ☆ ☆ ☆   Difficulty ☆ ☆ ☆ ☆ ☆

Equipment Changes

Position Changes

Notes

Cycling LOG BOOK

Date _____

Start Time _____

End Time _____

Weather

Day Mon ○ Tue ○ Wed ○ Thu ○ Fri ○ Sat ○ Sun ○

Route

⚷ Total Distance	🕐 Total Time	⌒ Average Speed

Route Rating

Road Condition ☆ ☆ ☆ ☆ ☆   Difficulty ☆ ☆ ☆ ☆ ☆

Equipment Changes

Position Changes

Notes

Cycling LOG BOOK

Date _____

Start Time _____

End Time _____

Day Mon ○ Tue ○ Wed ○ Thu ○ Fri ○ Sat ○ Sun ○

Weather

Route

🚴 Total Distance	🕐 Total Time	☁ Average Speed

Route Rating

Road Condition ☆ ☆ ☆ ☆ ☆

Difficulty ☆ ☆ ☆ ☆ ☆

Equipment Changes

Position Changes

Notes

Cycling LOG BOOK

Date _____

Start Time _____

End Time _____

Day Mon ○ Tue ○ Wed ○ Thu ○ Fri ○ Sat ○ Sun ○

Weather

Route

🦴 Total Distance	🕐 Total Time	🔺 Average Speed

Route Rating

Road Condition ☆ ☆ ☆ ☆ ☆   Difficulty ☆ ☆ ☆ ☆ ☆

Equipment Changes

Position Changes

Notes

Cycling LOG BOOK

Date _____

Start Time _____

End Time _____

Weather

Day Mon ○ Tue ○ Wed ○ Thu ○ Fri ○ Sat ○ Sun ○

Route

🦶 Total Distance	🕐 Total Time	⛱ Average Speed

Route Rating

Road Condition ☆ ☆ ☆ ☆ ☆   Difficulty ☆ ☆ ☆ ☆ ☆

Equipment Changes

Position Changes

Notes

Cycling LOG BOOK

Date _____

Start Time _____

End Time _____

Weather

Day: Mon ○ Tue ○ Wed ○ Thu ○ Fri ○ Sat ○ Sun ○

Route

Total Distance	Total Time	Average Speed

Route Rating

Road Condition ☆ ☆ ☆ ☆ ☆

Difficulty ☆ ☆ ☆ ☆ ☆

Equipment Changes

Position Changes

Notes

Cycling LOG BOOK

Date _____

Start Time _____

End Time _____

Weather

Day Mon ○ Tue ○ Wed ○ Thu ○ Fri ○ Sat ○ Sun ○

Route

🚲 Total Distance	🕐 Total Time	☁ Average Speed

Route Rating

Road Condition ☆ ☆ ☆ ☆ ☆   Difficulty ☆ ☆ ☆ ☆ ☆

Equipment Changes

Position Changes

Notes

Cycling LOG BOOK

Date _____

Start Time _____

End Time _____

Day Mon ○ Tue ○ Wed ○ Thu ○ Fri ○ Sat ○ Sun ○

Route

🔗 Total Distance	🕐 Total Time	🔽 Average Speed

Route Rating

Road Condition ☆ ☆ ☆ ☆ ☆   Difficulty ☆ ☆ ☆ ☆ ☆

Equipment Changes

Position Changes

Notes

Cycling LOG BOOK

Date _____

Start Time _____

End Time _____

Weather

Day Mon○ Tue○ Wed○ Thu○ Fri○ Sat○ Sun○

Route

Total Distance	Total Time	Average Speed

Route Rating

Road Condition ☆☆☆☆☆   Difficulty ☆☆☆☆☆

Equipment Changes

Position Changes

Notes

Cycling LOG BOOK

Date _____

Start Time _____

End Time _____

Day Mon ○ Tue ○ Wed ○ Thu ○ Fri ○ Sat ○ Sun ○

Route

Total Distance

Total Time

Average Speed

Route Rating

Road Condition ☆ ☆ ☆ ☆ ☆

Difficulty ☆ ☆ ☆ ☆ ☆

Equipment Changes

Position Changes

Notes

Cycling LOG BOOK

Date _____

Weather

Start Time _____

End Time _____

Day Mon ○ Tue ○ Wed ○ Thu ○ Fri ○ Sat ○ Sun ○

Route

🚴 Total Distance	🕐 Total Time	🔺 Average Speed

Route Rating

Road Condition ☆ ☆ ☆ ☆ ☆   Difficulty ☆ ☆ ☆ ☆ ☆

Equipment Changes

Position Changes

Notes

Cycling LOG BOOK

Date _____

Start Time _____

End Time _____

Weather

🌡 _____   ☀ ⛅ 🌧 ⛈ ❄

🚩 _____   ☐ ☐ ☐ ☐ ☐

Day: Mon ○ Tue ○ Wed ○ Thu ○ Fri ○ Sat ○ Sun ○

Route

🚲 Total Distance	🕐 Total Time	🔽 Average Speed

Route Rating

Road Condition ☆ ☆ ☆ ☆ ☆   Difficulty ☆ ☆ ☆ ☆ ☆

Equipment Changes

Position Changes

Notes

Cycling LOG BOOK

Date _____

Start Time _____

End Time _____

Weather

Day: Mon ○ Tue ○ Wed ○ Thu ○ Fri ○ Sat ○ Sun ○

Route

🚲 Total Distance	🕐 Total Time	☁ Average Speed

Route Rating

Road Condition ☆ ☆ ☆ ☆ ☆

Difficulty ☆ ☆ ☆ ☆ ☆

Equipment Changes

Position Changes

Notes

Made in the USA
Monee, IL
21 October 2021